Did ...

K...

A MISCELLANY

Compiled by Julia Skinner

With particular reference to the work of Paul Harris,
Keith Howell and Helen Livingston

THE FRANCIS FRITH COLLECTION

www.francisfrith.com

First published in the United Kingdom in 2010 by The Francis Frith Collection®

This edition published in 2014
ISBN 978-1-84589-817-5

British Library Cataloguing in Publication Data

Did You Know? Kent - A Miscellany
Compiled by Julia Skinner
With particular reference to the work of Paul Harris, Keith Howell and Helen Livingston

The Francis Frith Collection
6 Oakley Business Park,
Wylye Road, Dinton,
Wiltshire SP3 5EU
Tel: +44 (0) 1722 716 376
Email: info@francisfrith.co.uk
www.francisfrith.com

Printed and bound in England

Front Cover: **GOUDHURST, HOP PICKERS 1904** 52569p
Frontispiece: **ASHFORD, CHILDREN 1903** 50331v

The colour-tinting is for illustrative purposes only, and is not intended to be historically accurate

AS WITH ANY HISTORICAL DATABASE, THE FRANCIS FRITH ARCHIVE IS CONSTANTLY BEING
CORRECTED AND IMPROVED, AND THE PUBLISHERS WOULD WELCOME INFORMATION ON
OMISSIONS OR INACCURACIES

CONTENTS

INTRODUCTION

Kent ranks ninth in size amongst the counties of England, and perhaps no other county has more history within its boundaries. Separated from Europe by only 21 miles of sea, it has been invaded by foreign powers over the centuries. It has also been the target of several failed invasions from the time of the Napoleonic Wars in the early 19th century to 1940, when Hitler's invasion plans during the Second World War envisaged landing on the Kent coast. The many castles and other fortifications in Kent bear witness to conflict and turmoil in the past, but there are also glorious churches, the result of more peaceful energies, and two historic cathedrals, at Rochester and Canterbury.

Until the early 19th century, settlement in Kent was mainly rural, in small communities. In 1821 only one-fifth of the county's population lived in one of the 12 main towns. Thus the past has bequeathed a landscape of independent farmsteads, hamlets and rural villages. Although much agricultural land in Kent is under the plough nowadays, there are still areas of the orchards for which the county was once so famous, and also of hop gardens and their associated oast houses, so typical of Kent's landscape of the past. Hops were first introduced into England by Flemish weavers in the late 16th century. In the days when beer was a staple drink for much of the country's population there was a great demand for hops from the brewers, and hop growing was once a major industry of Kent.

Kent has over 126 miles of coastline, with the great advantages of good communications to the large centres of population around London, and generally warm, dry summers. The development of the railways in the mid 19th century changed the county; the lines stretched out from London to the nearest stretches of coastline, and in 1851 four of the ten largest seaside resorts in Britain were located in Kent – Margate, Ramsgate, Dover and Gravesend. In the next few decades the resorts of Broadstairs, Folkestone, Herne Bay and Deal also grew up as popular holiday destinations. Thus tourism became as important to Kent as the county's oast houses, orchards, castles, agriculture and historic cathedrals.

With new and improving transport routes to the county like the Channel Tunnel, the new rail link and the widening of the A2 in north Kent, the number of visitors arriving in the Garden of England increases every year. It is ironic to think, then, how long ago the people of Kent once fought off invaders. Today they reap the benefits of such high visitor numbers and they have a reason to embrace their home county's popularity with pride. With so much to see, to enjoy and most importantly to learn here, Kent continues to flourish; it retains a unique identity of its own – an identity that plays a major part in the socio-economic and cultural welfare of England today.

HERNE BAY, THE PARADE AND CLOCK TOWER 1889 22313

KENT DIALECT WORDS

'Chimleys' – chimneys.

'Crawlybob' – a woodlouse.

'Flittermouse' – a bat.

'Howsomever' – however.

'Huffkin' – a type of soft bread roll.

'Pinchywig' – an earwig.

'Pom' – jam.

'Strig' – the stalk of a flower or fruit.

'Wirretin' – worrying or fussing over something.

It has been claimed that the term 'to canter' used in horseriding may have originated from medieval pilgrims to Canterbury spurring their horses on to the faster 'Canterbury pace' of a gentle gallop as evening drew near, so that they could reach the city before its gates were shut for the night.

HAUNTED KENT

There are many ghost stories around Kent. Here are just a few:

Pluckley has the reputation of Britain's most haunted village. Amongst other apparitions, a 'lady in white' is said to throw herself from the bell tower of the 13th-century church of St Nicholas at midnight, and a 'lady in red' is supposed to drift around the churchyard – her figure was seen by one witness passing clean though a gravestone.

The Chequers Inn at Smarden is reputedly haunted by the phantom of a French prisoner of war from the past, who was lodged at the inn and murdered there. As recently as September 1997, a guest saw a small dark man who faded away when spoken to.

Offshore from Deal is the treacherous sandbank of the Goodwin Sands, which has caused more than 2,000 shipwrecks, including that of the 'Lady Lovibond' in February 1748; according to legend, the first mate deliberately steered the ship onto the sandbank in a fit of jealous rage because the captain had brought his new bride on board, with whom he was also in love. The 'Lady Lovibond' is said to reappear near the Goodwin Sands every 50 years from the date it was wrecked, as a ghost ship. The first sighting of the phantom ship, in 1798, was reported by two separate vessels; a sighting in 1848 appeared so real that a lifeboat was sent out to look for survivors; she was seen again in 1898, and then in 1948, when a ship's captain described the vessel as having an eerie green glow; however, there was no reported sighting when it was next due, in 1998.

The ghost of 'Lady Vain' is said to gallop around the village of Plaxtol on a phantom white horse; some residents have also reported hearing the sound of her singing in an eerie, high-pitched voice on summer evenings.

The ghost of Henry VIII's executed second wife, Anne Boleyn, is said to return to her childhood home of Hever Castle on Christmas Eve and crosses the bridge over the River Eden in the castle grounds.

KENT MISCELLANY

Kent is named after the Celtic tribe of the Cantiaci that lived in the area at the time of the Roman conquest of Britain in the first century AD.

Gravesend lies on the south bank of the River Thames; at this point the Thames narrows to become a London river, and coastal pilots hand over to the river men for the 26 miles further upstream to London Bridge. In Victorian times Gravesend became a popular resort, and the Thames barges and the local bawley boats that trawled for shrimps in the estuary, along with views of the ships of all nationalities passing on the river, were a source of interest for its visitors.

The massive keep of Rochester Castle was constructed in 1127, and is the tallest in the country. Conversely, Rochester's cathedral is one of the smallest in the country. The present building was mainly constructed in the 12th to the 14th centuries. Like Canterbury Cathedral, it is unusual in having double transepts, along with a raised choir and presbytery with a large crypt beneath.

**GRAVESEND
THE CLOCK TOWER
1902** 49026

ROCHESTER, HIGH STREET 1908 59875

The author Charles Dickens knew Rochester well, and the 16th-century Eastgate House in the High Street featured as the Westgate Seminary for Young Ladies in 'The Pickwick Papers'. The black and white timbered building opposite Eastgate House featured in 'Great Expectations' by Dickens as Mr Pumblechook's premises, where the hero, Pip, had an attic room. In 1856 Charles Dickens purchased Gad's Hill Place at Higham, near Rochester, where he lived until his death in 1870. The house is now a private school.

The monument overlooking the Medway Towns from Higham near Telegraph Hill commemorates Charles Larkin of Rochester (died 1826), who campaigned for an extension of the electoral franchise. His monument was placed at the highest point of the area, 'that all travellers in this district might behold a memento of one who had fought so nobly for Reform'.

Chatham was first developed in the 16th century as a base for Henry VIII's Tudor warships, and later a large dockyard and arsenal were established there. Of the many ships built at Chatham Dockyard, the most famous of them all was the 'Victory', launched in 1765; she was the flagship for successive admirals both before and after Lord Nelson was killed aboard her at the battle of Trafalgar in 1805. Throughout the 19th century Chatham continued to be the largest British naval shipbuilding yard. In 1863, the 'Achilles', the first armoured battleship built in a British royal dockyard, was launched there. The arrival of iron-hulled vessels introduced new technology and skills into shipbuilding and the dockyard site was increased in size. After 1908 the dockyard specialised in building and servicing submarines, and later had some involvement with nuclear submarines. Chatham's dockyard was closed in 1984, ending nearly 300 years of royal dockyard history. One part of the old dockyard, known as Chatham Maritime, has been redeveloped as an industrial and residential area, and the older, Georgian, part, Chatham Historic Dockyard, is now a maritime museum.

A TUDOR SHIP F6022

In the 1660s a naval dockyard was constructed at Sheerness as an extension to the dockyard at Chatham. The first houses at Sheerness were built by the dockyard construction workers for themselves to live in, using materials they were allowed to take from the dockyard. They painted the outside of the houses with the blue-grey naval paint they had access to, giving the area the name of 'Blue Houses', which later became 'Blue Town'. The north-west area of Sheerness is still known as Bluetown, although the original dockyard Blue Houses were destroyed in a fire in the 1820s. The Royal Navy ceased operating the dockyard in 1960, and the Bluetown area is now used for industrial purposes.

The four-storey Boat Store of Sheerness dockyard was completed in 1860 and was the world's first multi-storey iron-framed structure, making it the direct forerunner of modern skyscraper buildings. It is still standing today, and is Grade I listed. The frame of the building relies for its stability on joint stiffness rather than bracing.

Queenborough on the Isle of Sheppey gained its name in 1366, when Edward III gave the borough and port to his consort, Queen Phillippa.

Sittingbourne was an important market town in the past, from where Kent produce was transported on barges to the Thames and the London markets. This developed a barge-building and repairing industry in the area, a heritage recalled with a bronze statue of a bargeman in Sittingbourne's town centre and the Dolphin Sailing Barge Museum on the outskirts of the town, which tells the history of Thames Barges.

The ancient castle at Chilham was replaced in the 17th century by the present mansion, which has spacious grounds set out by John Tradescant, and later by 'Capability' Brown, that contain the first wisteria and mulberry tree ever to be planted in Britain. Only the keep of the old castle now remains, reputedly haunted by a ghostly 'grey lady'.

Beneath the streets of modern-day Canterbury are the remains of the Roman town of Cantiacorum Durovernum. In St Margaret's Street, part of the hypocaust, or under-floor heating system, of the bath complex of the Roman town is on show on the basement floor of the Waterstone's bookshop. The Roman Museum in Canterbury has been built around the remains of a Roman town house that was discovered beneath the Longmarket shopping development. The house had several rooms and corridors with colourful mosaic floors, some of which can be seen in the museum. In the museum are two rare Roman cavalry swords that were found in the city in 1970 – very few examples of cavalry swords have been found in Britain.

After the end of the Roman period, Kent was settled by Germanic invaders from the North Sea coast and Denmark. A kingdom of Kent emerged, with 'Cantwarabyrig' ('the burg, or defended settlement, of the Kentish people'), as its capital – which name later became Canterbury. In the late 6th century Pope Gregory sent a mission to England to convert the Anglo-Saxon people to Christianity, led by Augustine (later St Augustine). He and his companions landed in Kent and made for Cantwarabyrig to meet King Ethelbert whose wife, Bertha, a Frankish princess, was already a practising Christian; Queen Bertha worshipped in St Martin's Church in Canterbury, which probably dates back to a Christian church founded there during the Roman period and is the oldest parish church in England where Christian worship has taken place continuously. King Ethelbert was baptised as a Christian on Whit Sunday, AD597.

Long stretches of Canterbury's medieval city walls are still visible – the best sections can be seen at Dane John and Broad Street. The massive twin-towered West Gate, seen in photograph C18047, opposite, is the only survivor of the medieval gates which once interrupted the path of the defensive wall around the city – all but West Gate were pulled down in the 1780s.

Canterbury is famous for its magnificent cathedral of which St Augustine was the first archbishop, having founded it in AD602. The present building was founded by the Normans in 1070, replacing the earlier Anglo-Saxon cathedral, but the nave was rebuilt between 1378 and 1405 and the sublime crossing tower that we see today, now known as Bell Harry Tower, was designed by John Wastell, the King's Master Mason, who worked on it from the mid 15th century to 1503 (see photograph 21359 on page 49). Bell Harry Tower is named after the original bell that was given for the central tower of the cathedral in 1316 by Prior Henry (Harry) Eastry to summon the congregation to services, and Bell Harry still functions as a 'calling bell' today, sited in a frame on top of the tower.

CANTERBURY, WEST GATE AND ST DUNSTAN'S STREET c1955
C18047

CANTERBURY, THE WEAVERS' HOUSE c1955 C18104

From the late 16th century a number of Huguenots and Walloons fled from religious persecution in France and Flanders and came to England, bringing with them their weaving skills. Some came to Canterbury, and the Weavers' House in the High Street (now a restaurant) was the centre of much of their industry, seen in photograph C181104, above. It once housed hundreds of looms, and the River Stour below it was used in part of the cloth-making process. Near the Weavers' House is a modern replica of the ducking stool that was used in medieval times to punish nagging women by ducking them in the river, seen in the background of the photograph.

In 1170 Thomas Becket, Archbishop of Canterbury, was murdered in Canterbury Cathedral by four of Henry II's knights. There had been a long dispute over control of the Church between Archbishop Becket and Henry II, and the knights had over-zealously interpreted the king's angry outburst of 'Will no one rid me of this turbulent priest!' when his exasperation with the stubborn archbishop boiled over. Thomas Becket was canonised in 1173, and the shrine of St Thomas became one of the most popular pilgrimage destinations of medieval Europe, immortalised by Geoffrey Chaucer (1335-1400) in his 'Canterbury Tales' about a group of pilgrims travelling to Canterbury from Southwark.

After a major fire in Canterbury Cathedral in 1174, the choir was rebuilt spectacularly (see photograph 70340, below). It was designed by William of Sens, a French master mason skilled in the Gothic style of northern France, with its pointed arches and universal stone-built ribbed vaults. William of Sens fell from scaffolding during construction and returned to France, and the work was completed by another William, 'the Englishman'. Construction began in 1175 and finished in 1184. William the Englishman was responsible for the design of the Trinity Chapel, which housed the shrine of St Thomas Becket, and the Corona Tower at its eastern end, where St Thomas's crown (the top of his skull) was kept, which was severed by the swords of his murderers. The magnificent shrine of St Thomas in the cathedral was destroyed at the Reformation in 1538, and nowadays a lighted candle marks the place where it once stood.

**CANTERBURY
CATHEDRAL
THE CHOIR
LOOKING
EAST 1921**
70340

13

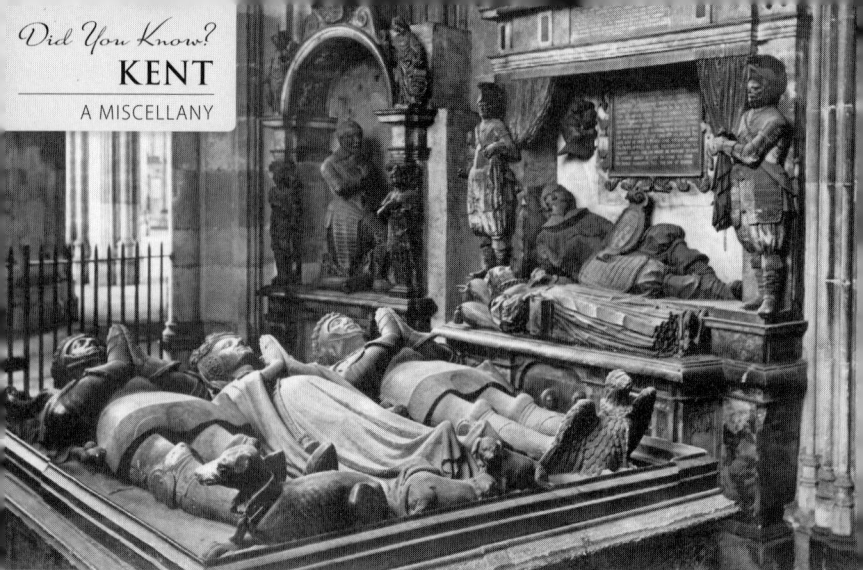

The Canterbury-born artist T S (Sidney) Cooper (1803-1902) was famous for his paintings of pastoral scenes, especially for his depictions of cattle. A gallery at the Royal Museum and Art Gallery in Canterbury is devoted to his work. The Sidney Cooper Gallery in St Peter's Street in the city was originally an art school founded by the artist in 1882. One person who studied there was Mary Tourtel, born in Canterbury in 1874, who created the famous cartoon character of Rupert Bear; he is now the subject of his own museum in the city, the Rupert Bear Museum in Stour Street.

St Mary's Church at Reculver was built on the former site of the Roman fortress of Regulbium, established around AD280 to guard the Wantsum Channel. Erosion of the coastline prompted the demolition of most of the church in 1809, leaving only its 12th-century twin towers, known locally as 'The Two Sisters', which were restored as a navigational aid. An old legend said that on stormy nights the sound of crying babies could be heard in the area; some basis for this story was found when archaeologists excavating the Roman fort found a number of babies' skeletons, but why they were buried there will now never be known.

RECULVER, THE TOWERS
1892 31457

MARGATE, THE SANDS 1906   54758

Margate was developed in the mid 18th century as the earliest coastal and sea-bathing resort, with many visitors travelling there on Margate 'hoys', flat-bottomed boats which carried both passengers and cargo along the coast and on the Thames. From this came the nautical cry of 'Ahoy', used to hail a hoy to stop and take on a passenger. Bathing machines are said to have been invented by a Margate man, Benjamin Beale, in the 1750s as somewhere for ladies to change into their bathing apparel and conserve their modesty whilst they took a dip in the sea. These small huts on wheels would be hauled or backed into the sea by horses, and the ladies wishing to bathe then disembarked down steps at the rear, protected from cold winds and inquisitive stares by a canvas hood attached to the back of the vehicle. Margate also lays claim to have been the first seaside resort to have used donkey rides as an amusement. From about 1800 a Mr Bennett in the High Street kept donkeys for hire at a shilling an hour.

The terrace of houses along the short road of Buenos Ayres near the seafront in Margate was built in 1806. The unusual Spanish name is said to reflect the fact that the Argentine city of Buenos Ayres had been captured by a British invasion force in that year.

Broadstairs was originally a fishing village known as 'Bradstow'. It was noted for the cliff-top shrine of 'Our Lady of Bradstow', so venerated by sailors that they would dip their sails in salute as they passed. 'Bradstow' was an Old English form of the words 'broad stairs', which alluded to the stairs that in the 14th century were cut into the cliffs leading from the beach to the shrine and later became the name of the town. The archway in Broadstairs shown in photograph 19726 (below) was once fitted with a portcullis and gates as a protection against pirates and sea-raiders. It was first built in the 16th century in a bid to protect the shipyard in nearby Harbour Street from attack, and was then called the Flint Gate; it was re-built in 1795 and re-named the York Gate after Prince Frederick, the 'Grand Old Duke of York' (1763–1827), who was the Commander-in-Chief of the British Army during the French Revolutionary and Napoleonic Wars.

Charles Dickens bought a property in Broadstairs overlooking the bay that was then known as Fort House (now Bleak House), and spent holidays there for many years. Dickens loved this house, and called it his 'airy nest'; it was there that he wrote 'David Copperfield'.

BROADSTAIRS THE YORK GATE 1887
19726

**RAMSGATE
THE HARBOUR CROSSWALL
1907** 58287

Ramsgate harbour was constructed in 1749-91 following a disastrous storm. The outer harbour was created as a 'harbour of refuge' to provide a safe haven for shipping in bad weather; the West Pier lighthouse has the Latin words 'perfugium miseris' cut into the stonework below its lantern, which means 'shelter for the distressed'. In 1821 George IV used Ramsgate as his point of embarkation and return for a journey to Hanover, and was so pleased with the warm reception he was given by the local people that he decreed that Ramsgate harbour be a 'Royal Harbour'. An obelisk near the harbour commemorates this – it is known locally as the Royal Toothpick.

On the left of photograph 58297 (opposite) of Pegwell are the Floral Tea Gardens, followed by the Pear Tree Inn, which was later Samuel Banger's potted shrimp paste factory. His small paste pots had highly decorated lids depicting scenes of Pegwell; today they are valuable antiques.

Deal Castle, shown in photograph 76073 on page 21, was erected in Tudor times as part of the coastal fortifications, the largest of three fortresses built by Henry VIII in 1538 to protect this stretch of Kent coast against the threat of French invasion – the other two were at Walmer and Sandgate. Six semi-circular bastions fan out from a round central keep with gun emplacements facing in all directions, all surrounded by a massive moat.

The ancient two-cell late Norman church of St Nicholas at Barfrestone is renowned for its 'wagon wheel' rose window and the amazing, exuberant stone carvings that cover its exterior, which depict aspects of medieval life. An unusual feature is that the church's bell is attached to a yew tree in the churchyard, as the building has no tower.

PEGWELL, HIGH STREET 1907 58297

The Saxon name of Sandwich means 'the settlement on the sandbank'. Sandwich was once a Cinque Port at the mouth of the River Stour, but owing to silting it is now two miles from the sea. Sandwich retains two of its ancient town gates, Barbican Gate (or Bridgegate) and Fisher Gate. The Barbican was not originally a proper gateway to the town, but part of the outer defensive works. It was constructed in 1539, with semi-circular flanking bastions, as one of a chain of blockhouses built by Henry VIII as part of England's coastal defences. It later became the residence of the keepers of the toll bridge, and all traffic to Thanet passed under its arches, where a toll was paid.

In 1457 a French force from Honfleur attacked Sandwich and laid waste to parts of the town. Many citizens were killed, including the mayor, John Drury. From that time on, successive mayors of Sandwich have always worn black ceremonial robes in memory of the event, a tradition that has continued to this day, despite attempts by Honfleur (now twinned with Sandwich) to persuade the town to drop the custom.

SANDWICH, THE BARBICAN 1894 34210

DEAL, THE CASTLE 1924 76073

In Roman times the estuary of the River Dour at Dover was used as a harbour, and the Roman fleet in Britain, the 'Classis Britannica', was based there for a while. Standing within the walls of Dover Castle is the shell of the octagonal 'pharos', or lighthouse, that the Romans erected as a beacon for their galleys. The mouth of the River Dour silted up in the Middle Ages, and various artificial harbours for Dover had to be constructed instead.

In 1970 the remains of a Roman 'mansio' (a hostel for government officials) were discovered at Dover, dating from c200. Dubbed the Roman Painted House, the building contained some for the finest examples of Roman painted plaster murals in Britain. Parts of 28 painted panels have survived, each with a motif associated with Bacchus, the Roman god of wine and intoxication. The remains of the Roman Painted House have now been preserved as a visitor attraction, located in New Street in Dover.

DOVER, THE PROMENADE 1908 60393

The white cliffs of Dover have long symbolised Britain's determination to repel invaders, and one of the finest fortresses in the country, Dover Castle, dominates the town and the harbour. The great keep, the inner bailey and much of the curtain walling of the present stronghold were built by Henry II between 1168-86 at a colossal cost. Further additions to the defences were made by Henry III (1216-72), and also during the Napoleonic Wars, and again in the Second World War. Dover Castle was still used by the Army up until the late 1950s.

Between Dover and Folkestone is the entrance to the Channel Tunnel at Cheriton. Work on the tunnel started in 1988 and finished in 1998. A total of 95 miles of tunnelling was completed by a workforce of nearly 13,000, running under the Channel to Sangatte in France, near Calais. Spoil excavated from the tunnel during its construction was transferred to a site on the Kent coast between Dover and Folkestone, where it forms a convincing chalk cliff coastline called Samphire Hoe. This is now a nature reserve where many rare chalk plants grow, which attract a wealth of butterflies and other insects.

The Old Town of Folkestone is based around the steep, narrow streets of the fishing harbour, and the extensive seaside resort was developed in Victorian times, after the arrival of the railway. Photograph 48054 (below) shows a view of The Leas at Folkestone taken from the Victoria Pier, which was demolished in 1954. The Leas was patrolled by the local landowner Lord Radnor's own policemen during the late 19th and early 20th centuries. They would keep 'undesirables' off the elegant promenade, even turning away people they considered to be dressed inappropriately. To the right of the photograph the water-balanced lift can be seen, which still saves holidaymakers the bother of climbing to the top of the cliff.

There are a number of places in Folkestone with the name Bouverie, such as Bouverie Place. These commemorate Jacon de Bouverie, who became Lord of the Manor in 1697, and who was the first to produce a detailed map of the town.

FOLKESTONE, THE LEAS FROM THE PIER 1901 48054

Photograph 35528 (below) shows the statue of William Harvey in Folkestone. Dr Harvey was born in a house in Church Street in the town in 1578, now marked with a plaque, and eventually became court physician to the king (James I initially, then Charles I). In 1628 Dr Harvey published his revolutionary theory explaining how blood circulates around the body through the network of arteries, veins and capillaries, the achievement for which he is most remembered. William Harvey died in 1657, and money left in his will helped to found a free school in Folkestone, now known as the Harvey Grammar School.

Road of Remembrance in Folkestone is so called because in 1915, during the First World War, Folkestone became the main port of embarkation for troops going off to fight on the Continent. As many as 7 million men may have marched down this road, many never to return, hence the name.

**FOLKESTONE, CASTLE HILL AVENUE AND THE HARVEY STATUE
1895** 35528

During the Napoleonic Wars a series of 74 Martello Towers were built along the south coast of England to protect it against invasion; 27 of these squat, round towers with extra thick walls on the seaward side were built along the Kent coast between 1805-1808, of which 16 survive, with 9 at Folkestone. A cannon atop each tower could fire a 24lb shot for a mile. Martello Tower design was based on a fort at Cape Mortella on Corsica, which impressed the Royal Navy by its impregnability.

During the Second World War, the crucially important Battle of Britain was fought in the skies over Kent from 10th June until 31st October 1940, when the German Luftwaffe finally accepted it could not defeat the RAF. Three thousand aircrew flew under Fighter Command, and of them 507 lost their lives. Hawkinge, just outside Folkestone, is the home of the Kent Battle of Britain Museum, containing replica Spitfires, Hurricanes and Messerschmidts among other artefacts. At nearby Capel-le-Ferne is the Battle of Britain Memorial. This takes the form of a huge three-bladed propeller set into the ground, with the statue of a lone pilot at its centre. The RAF Memorial Flight passes over the memorial on the nearest Sunday to 10th July each year.

On 28th April 2007, south-east Kent was shaken by an earthquake that registered 4.3 on the Richter scale. The worst affected area was Folkestone (the epicentre of the earthquake was just north of the town), but Deal, Dover and Ashford also felt its effects. Hundreds of properties in Folkestone were damaged, many so seriously that people could not return to them, but luckily no one was killed. The Folkestone area was shaken by a further tremor on 3rd March 2009, although this was less serious, measuring 3.0 on the Richter scale.

Hythe was once one of the Cinque Ports, but the sea receded and the quay ended up half a mile inland. Most of Hythe's parish church of St Leonard dates from the 13th century, but the tower was destroyed in an earthquake in 1739, and rebuilt in 1750. It is often described as a 'herring church', built when the Cinque Ports enjoyed prosperity from the herring harvest from the sea. Its most remarkable feature is the magnificent Early English chancel, set higher than the rest of the church and richly embellished with carved mouldings, multiple pier shafts and a stone vaulted ceiling.

Between 1804 and 1809, as part of the defences established during the Napoleonic Wars to protect the south coast, the 28-mile-long Royal Military Canal was constructed from Seabrook, near Hythe, to Winchelsea in Sussex. The canal's function was to be an obstacle for invaders and also a means to transport goods, supplies and troops. The Royal Military Canal now divides the modern seaside resort of Hythe from the old town, and Hythe celebrates its canal with the popular summer Venetian Fete every other year, with colourful floating tableaux, illuminated floats and firework displays.

The Romney, Hythe and Dymchurch Railway opened in 1927 and is the world's smallest public railway service. From Hythe to New Romney the 15-inch gauge line is double tracked, so trains travelling in the opposite direction can pass each other. However, beyond New Romney the line is a single track to Dungeness with a passing place at Romney Sands. It is still running today, and serves both as a novelty for holidaymakers and as a commuter train for local schoolchildren.

The Romney Marsh is a region of flat wetland that encompasses an area near the coast over west Kent and East Sussex. It was reclaimed from the sea in ancient times. The Romans farmed here and constructed massive dykes that still perform a role in safeguarding the region's interests. The first recorded tenancy of land on the Romney Marsh was granted to a man called Baldwin in the 12th century, allowing him the use of 'as much land as Baldwin himself can enclose and drain against the sea'; his drainage ditch is still in use, known as 'Baldwin's Sewer'. In the 19th century the pastures of the marsh supported huge numbers of sheep, and a specific breed developed here, the Romney Marsh, which is able to feed and thrive in wet situations and is more resistant than other breeds to foot rot, caused by being kept on damp land. During the 20th century the area was home to the author Russell Thorndike, who based a famous series of novels featuring the smuggling character of Dr Syn in Dymchurch and the Romney Marsh.

For many centuries Ashford was a small country town with a busy weekly market. Ashford's main expansion came with the arrival of the railway in 1842, after which it became an important rail junction with routes in five directions, and also a centre of engine and rolling stock manufacture for the South Eastern Railway. The railway works opened in 1847, the same year that the SER started building a model village nearby to accommodate their employees. This model village was originally called Alfred, but later became known as Newtown. In 1962 all locomotive production and repairs were moved away from Ashford to Eastleigh, but the town's important railway heritage is commemorated with the fountain in Lower High Street in the town, with a railway engine wheel at its heart.

During the First World War, Ashford citizens took part in fundraising to help the war effort, and the scale of their success was recognised after the war. Towns that did well with fundraising were given a redundant tank in recognition of their success. Other towns that received a tank have long since disposed of theirs, but Ashford still has its tank on display. This Mark IV tank was driven into its position in St George's Square in the town in 1919. It has since had its guns and engines removed, and for many years it contained an electricity sub-station.

ASHFORD, HIGH STREET 1906 53444

The village of Bethersden was once well-known for the quarrying of 'Bethersden Marble', a coarse, hard limestone containing small fossilised crustaceans; apart from being used locally, it was used for interior work in both Canterbury and Rochester cathedrals, and in a number of local medieval churches.

In the parish church of St Mary at Great Chart are a number of memorial brasses to six local men who together married a total of fifteen wives; two of them each married no less than five times. They include Captain Nicholas Toke, who set out at the age of ninety-three to walk to London in 1680 to find a sixth bride, but died before encountering her.

Tenterden prospered in the Middle Ages on sheep, wool and weaving. Its fine parish church is unusual in that it is dedicated to St Mildred, a Saxon princess who was abbess of the abbey at Minster-in-Thanet and canonised after her death in AD732. From 1830 to 1859 the vicar of St Mildred's was Reverend Philip Ward, whose wife Horatia was the daughter of Lord Nelson and Lady Hamilton. The William Caxton pub in Tenterden is named after the first English printer, believed to have been born in or near the town around 1422 (although Hadlow near Tonbridge also claims to have been his birthplace). William Caxton learned the art of printing whilst working abroad, then returned to his homeland and produced the first book ever printed in England, 'Dictes or Sayengis of the Philosophres' in London in 1477.

By the 14th century, a shipbuilding industry was developing at the Smallhythe area of Tenterden. The River Rother in those days flowed both north and south of the Isle of Oxney, and the northern branch was sufficiently deep for ships to be built and launched at Smallhythe; the area became the premier shipbuilding location in the country until the late 16th century when the silting-up of the Rother ended the industry. The 15th-century timbered cottage known as Smallhythe Place was the harbour-master's house in medieval times. From 1899 to 1928 Smallhythe Place was the home of the famous actress Ellen Terry, and it is now in the care of the National Trust as a memorial to her; amongst other things it contains a wonderful collection of her theatrical costumes.

The parish church of St Mary the Virgin at Rolvenden contains an oddity: a squire's pew situated at first floor level over the south chapel, furnished with a carpet, table and Chippendale chairs.

In medieval times Biddenden was the home of the Biddenden Maids, Elisa and Mary Chulkhurst, who feature on the village sign. The Maids were Siamese twins who were born in the village joined together at the hips and shoulders, and lived like that for 34 years. When one died, the other refused to be separated, and died a few hours later. After their deaths, the sisters bequeathed their lands in trust for the village, the income to be spent on the sick and needy and also to provide a gift of bread and cheese for the poor on Easter Monday morning, known as the Biddenden Dole. This is still given out each year, although the bread and cheese now takes the form of a commemorative biscuit.

The village of Smarden's 15th-century parish church of St Michael is known as 'the barn of Kent' because of the width of its aisleless nave and the timber scissor-beam roof.

TENTERDEN, HIGH STREET 1900 44994

Cranbrook became the centre of cloth making in the county in the 14th century and the trade lasted until the 18th century; it was known for its fine, smooth woollen cloth called broadcloth, especially a variety called Cranbrook Grey. Cranbrook's typical Kentish architecture of weatherboarded houses is complemented by the Union Mill, the largest working windmill in England, seen in the background of photograph 56971 (below). Built in 1814 for Henry Dobell, the mill received its name because a union of local tradespeople ran it after Henry Dobell went bankrupt. One of Cranbrook's most distinctive buildings is the Providence Chapel in Stone Street, which was built in 1828. It has a seven-sided front made of timber, cleverly grooved to look like stone.

The castle at Sissinghurst is renowned for its gardens, designed in the 1930s by Vita Sackville-West as a series of 'rooms' around a different theme or colour scheme.

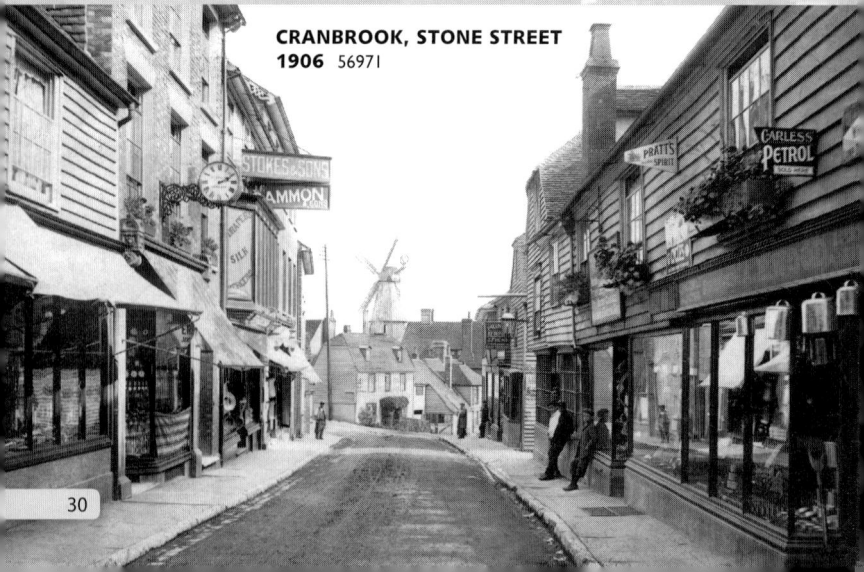

CRANBROOK, STONE STREET 1906 56971

Often called 'The Cathedral of the Weald', St Dunstan's Church in Cranbrook was built of local yellow sandstone in the mid 15th century, and restored during the 19th century. There are many interesting carved figures on the exterior of the church, and the south wall of the tower has an impressive clock, with the figure of Father Time and his scythe.

All Saints' Church in Staplehurst is famous for its south door, dated to 1050, which is decorated with wrought-iron Viking symbols that tell the story of Ragnarok, the Norse Day of Judgement. Amongst the motifs are the Ship of the Dead and the Midgard Serpent, depicted both wriggling in life and then stretched out in death, having been slain by the Norse god Thor; above them the dragon Nithhogr, that feeds on the slain, flies through the sky. On this fateful day Nature has been thrown into confusion, and other motifs show seals and fish that have come out of the sea to the land. But also shown on the door is a cross, symbolic of the new hope to follow as people turn from the old Norse gods to Christianity.

The village sign on the green at Bearsted shows the famous cricketer Alfred Mynn (1807-1861) at the wicket, wearing a top hat. Known as 'Mighty Mynn, the Lion of Kent', he lived in Ware Street in Bearsted and was a member of Bearsted Cricket Club, which celebrated its 250th anniversary in 1999. Regarded as one of the finest all-rounders the game had ever had, he was one of the first cricket players to master over-arm bowling.

The 15th-century church of the Holy Cross at Bearsted is remarkable for three sculptures of heraldic beasts that crouch at three corners of the top of its tower. Once thought to be three bears, and later three lions, they are now believed to represent a lion, a panther and a griffin. In the churchyard is the stump of a tree, all that remains of a Canadian cypress known as the Mourning Tree that marked the grave of John Dyke, who was hanged at Penenden Heath at Maidstone in 1830 for rick-burning. Years later, the man who had accused him of the crime admitted on his death bed that he had been the arsonist, and that John Dyke had been innocent.

Leeds, east of Maidstone, is famous for its stunning and romantic castle. For three centuries it was the dower home of eight medieval queens in succession, and was sometimes used as a prison for 'persons of consequence'. Much loved by Henry VIII, who lavished substantial sums on its improvement, it was then owned in turn by the St Leger, Culpeper and Fairfax families. The castle was left to the nation in 1974.

Kent's county town of Maidstone owes its importance to its position where the road from London to the coast crosses the River Medway, though the river was not bridged here until 1879, when Sir Joseph Bazalgette erected the original 'Great Bridge'. Until that time the Maidstone ferry was the only means of crossing the river. The important commercial artery of the Medway, 'the highway of Kent', was tidal as far upstream as East Farleigh until the 17th century when the river was controlled by sluices and locks. Until the middle years of the 20th century the Medway was plied by tan-sailed Thames barges with their cargoes of timber and paper, and by the 'stumpies', Medway narrow boats used by the Kentish brickworks.

It was on Penenden Heath near Maidstone in 1381 that recruits to the Peasants' Revolt elected Wat Tyler as their leader, and he led them into Maidstone. They released prisoners held in the jail in the town, including the wayward priest John Ball, before marching to London to confront the young King Richard II with their demands for the abolition of serfdom and the poll tax. However, Wat Tyler was struck down and killed at Smithfield by the mayor of London, the rebellion was crushed, and in Maidstone people were fined, had their homes destroyed and property confiscated as punishment for their part in it. Wat Tyler Way is the name that was given to a new road in Maidstone that crosses the River Len and links the Ashford and Sittingbourne roads with Mote Road and Knightrider Street. However, it was by way of Union Street, formerly Tyler's Lane, that the rebel leader is said to have entered the town during the Peasants' Revolt.

MAIDSTONE, MARKET PLACE 1885 12684

Clare Park in Maidstone, which opened in Tonbridge Road in 1923, was named for Lady Clare Sharp, the wife of local sweets maker Sir Edward Sharp.

In the Middle Ages, Maidstone was the site of the Archbishop of Canterbury's country residence. The former Archbishop's Palace stands beside the river in the town; this mainly 14th-century building is now used as the Kent Register Office. Maidstone's museum in St Faith's Street is housed in a splendid red-brick Tudor house that was once Chillington Manor, a home of the prominent Wyatt family whose ancestral seat was Allington Castle, near Maidstone. A member of the Wyatt family is commemorated in an interesting memorial in the Church of St Mary the Virgin and All Saints at Boxley, near Maidstone. Sir Henry Wyatt was imprisoned in the Tower of London in 1483 for denying Richard III's right to the crown. The memorial was put up by Edwin Wiat and reads: 'To the memory of Sir Henry Wiat, of Alington Castle, Knight banneret, descended of that ancient family, who was imprisoned and tortured in the Tower, in the reign of King Richard the third, kept in the dungeon, where fed and preserved by a cat…'. Sir Henry had been left cold and starving in his cell in the Tower, but he befriended a cat that found its way in and kept him company. The cat kept him warm by sleeping on his chest at night and brought him pigeons that it caught, which the warder agreed to cook for him to eat, thus saving his life.

Kentish ragstone, the distinctive grey sandstone of the Quarry Hills, has been quarried in the Maidstone area since Roman times. With its five arches, the ragstone bridge over the River Medway at East Farleigh is said to be the finest medieval bridge in the south of England. Another notable bridge in Kent is at Yalding, south-west of Maidstone, which boasts the longest surviving medieval bridge in the county, crossing two rivers over a span of 137 metres (150 yards).

To the west of the A229 near Aylesford is Kent's most famous Neolithic burial chamber, known as Kit's Coty House, which dates from around 5,000 years ago. The huge capstone is supported by three large uprights, and the stones were originally covered with an earthen mound. At the west end there used to be a large stone known as the General's Tombstone, but this was blown up in 1867 because it hampered farming; it was probably the last remnant of a ring of stones around the mound. It is said that this ancient monument is named after a local shepherd named Kit who used it as a shelter in the 17th century ('coty' means 'small house' in the local dialect), although there is another theory that the name derives from the Celtic 'ked koit', meaning 'the tomb in the wood'.

AYLESFORD, KIT'S COTY HOUSE 1898 41555

The 13th-century St George's Church at Wrotham (pronounced 'Rootum') stands right on the road on the north side of the village square. An unusual feature of the church is that a vaulted passageway extends from north to south beneath the foot of its tower, enabling processions to take place around the west end of the church without leaving consecrated ground. This would otherwise have been impossible, since the adjoining highway abuts the building. The church is famous for its medieval memorial brasses: there are fifty figures from five families, dating from 1498 to 1615. It also has one of the oldest working church clocks in the country, made in the early 17th century.

WROTHAM, THE VILLAGE AND ST GEORGE'S CHURCH 1904 52831

IGHTHAM, THE SQUARE 1901 47623

Ightham was anciently known as Eightham, and once held a Whit-Wednesday fair called Cockscomb Fair. Nearby is the 14th-century fortified manor house of Ightham Mote, one of the finest moated houses in England.

The parish church at Plaxtol is unusual in that it has never been dedicated to any saint. The church was built in 1649 during the Commonwealth period that followed the Civil War, and was given no patron saint in keeping with the Puritan ethics of that time.

SEVENOAKS, HIGH STREET 1900 44904

The name of Sevenoaks really does seem to mean 'seven oak trees'. The original trees probably grew in a clump near the parish church, and gave their name to the settlement there, but they had vanished by medieval times. The tradition of seven oak trees planted in a straight line along the main road to the south of the town dates from 1727, when a row of oak trees was planted alongside the Tonbridge turnpike road, the first row of seven oaks deliberately planted at Sevenoaks; they were felled in 1955 when it was mistakenly thought that they were diseased. The tradition of seven oak trees on the northern perimeter of the Vine, the open space on the north of the town, is even younger. The original oaks there were planted to celebrate the accession of Edward VII in 1901. Sadly, six of them were felled by the 1987 hurricane, but they have been replanted.

Near Sevenoaks is the great house of Knole. The original medieval buildings at Knole were sold in 1456 to the then Archbishop of Canterbury who built a palace in their place, and the open space known as The Vine at Sevenoaks is named after the archbishop's vineyard which used to stand there. The archbishop's palace passed to Thomas Sackville, Earl of Dorset in the early 1600s, who embellished it to be the magnificent Jacobean house that we see today. The house is said to possess 'a courtyard for every day of the week, a staircase for every week of the year, and a room for every day of the year'.

The green at Westerham is dominated by two statues of famous men in Britain's history. One is of General James Wolfe, famous for his victory over the French in Canada when he took Quebec in 1759; General Wolfe was born at what is now the Old Vicarage in Westerham and spent his childhood in the town at the 17th-century building now known as Quebec House. The other is of Sir Winston Churchill, Britain's Prime Minister during the Second World War, who lived at Chartwell Manor near Westerham.

Tonbridge grew beside a castle that was originally built in William the Conqueror's time to guard the ford there over the Medway on the London to south coast road; the castle was demolished in the Civil War, and only the 13th-century gatehouse remains. Some medieval buildings in the town survive, notably the Port Reeve's House in East Street and the Chequers Inn in the High Street, a half-timbered building that dates from the 15th century and is famous for its 'gallows' sign, projecting over the street.

A feature of Chiddingstone is the 'Chiding Stone' or 'Judgement Stone', a large sandstone boulder that provided a natural rostrum from which judgement may have been delivered in the past. Legend has it that scolding women and wrongdoers were brought here in the past to be 'chided' on the error of their ways and that the stone gave the village its name, but it is more likely to have originated from 'Ciddingas', meaning it was the homestead of the people of a Saxon leader named Cidd.

Hever is famous for its moated castle, which from 1462 to 1539 was the seat of the Boleyn (originally 'Bullen') family; Henry VIII's second wife Anne Boleyn spent part of her childhood here. Photograph 29396 (below) was taken twelve years before the castle was bought and restored by Lord Astor. Now open to the public, the castle gardens are magnificent and the square sandstone house, which dates from 1384, contains a marvellous collection of paintings and furniture.

Tunbridge Wells was once a scattered hamlet in a forested part of the Weald. But in 1606 a chalybeate (iron rich) spring was discovered in the area, visitors flocked there to take the waters for the good of their health, and Tunbridge Wells grew into a handsome spa town. A glass of Tunbridge Wells chalybeate spring water contains an average of 10 milligrams of iron.

HEVER, HEVER CASTLE 1891 29396

TUNBRIDGE WELLS, THE PANTILES c1890 T87001

In 1638 a promenade called the Walks was laid out at Tunbridge Wells, now known as the Pantiles, which is a terraced walk with shops behind a colonnade, flanked by lime trees. The Pantiles is a name that originates from the end of the 17th century. In 1698, Princess (later Queen) Anne visited the town with her husband Prince George of Denmark and their young son William, Duke of Gloucester. The young duke fell on the muddy walks and his mother provided the town with the sum of £100 for paving the area. Princess Anne returned the next year but the work had not started and she left the town in a fury, never to return. However, she did appoint a supervisor to oversee the paving, and in 1700 the Upper Walk was paved with square earthenware tiles that were pan-baked to ensure uniform size, known as pantiles, which gave the area its name.

Fine examples of items known as Tunbridge Ware can be seen in Tunbridge Wells Museum. Tunbridge Ware originated as basic wooden souvenirs sold to tourists from the 1680s. The earliest wares were undecorated turned articles but from 1750 more specialised manufacturers emerged, producing elaborate pieces decorated with printed designs, attached prints, marquetry or wooden mosaic designs. The items they made included boxes for sewing tools, toys, desks, tables, chests, bookshelves, stands, games boards, snuff boxes, miniature tea-sets and cutlery.

Paddock Wood has a place in motoring history as the scene of the first speeding offence that took place in Britain. Mr Walter Arnold of East Peckham was fined one shilling (5p) at Tonbridge Magistrates Court for travelling at 8mph in a 2mph area in Paddock Wood in 1896. He was caught by a policeman who had successfully chased him on a bicycle.

WATERINGBURY, MANOR FARM, OAST HOUSES c1960 W399024

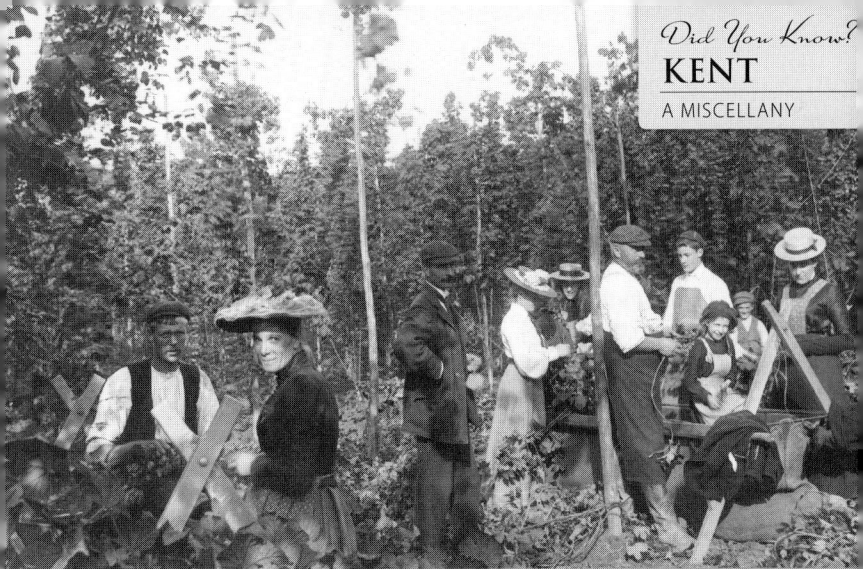

GOUDHURST, HOP PICKERS 1904 52569

A major part of Kent's economy in the past was the growing of hops, used for flavouring and preserving beer. Kent's hop growing past is commemorated by the Whitbread Hop Farm at Paddock Wood, the largest hop and oast complex ever built, and now a popular museum. Hops produce long stems each year, called 'bines', which appear in May and are trained up a trellis-work of poles and wires, to an overhead gantry of wire – this process is known as 'twiddling'. By mid-June the shoots reach the wire and flop over the top. In early September the hops are ready for picking. Harvesting the hops is now done by machines, but formerly, the cones were hand-picked by seasonal labourers, either local families or poor people from London taking an annual working holiday. The hops were then taken to the oast houses to be dried. The oast houses were basically kilns, or ovens, where the piles of hops were dried on sacking laid over wooden slats, and heated by fires of anthracite mixed with sulphur. The fumes escaped through the distinctively shaped cowls at the top. The hop-drying process has now been modernised, and many old oast houses are now used as storerooms or have been converted into houses.

St Mary's Church at Goudhurst holds many memorials to the Culpeper family. The fine alabaster monument shown in photograph 52540 (opposite) commemorates four generations of the family from Tudor times. At the top is the figure of Sir Thomas Culpeper, Sheriff of Kent in the reign of Edward VI. Beneath Sir Thomas is his son, Sir Alexander Culpeper, accompanied by his wife, Mary. The two kneeling figures in the centre of the row at the bottom are Sir Alexander's son, Anthony Culpeper and his wife Ann, and on each side are their sixteen children, kneeling in prayer.

In the 18th century the Star and Eagle Inn at Goudhurst was a centre for the notorious Hawkhurst Gang's smuggling trade, connected with the village church by a secret underground passage. Eventually the village had enough of the gang terrorising the area, and the Goudhurst Militia fought the 100-strong smuggling gang in a pitched battle in the churchyard on 20th April 1747 whilst the villagers took shelter within the church. The battle resulted in the deaths of three of the smugglers, including one of their leaders, and brought the activities of the gang to an end.

Hawkhurst was a centre of the Wealden iron industry from Roman times until the 18th century. In the 17th century one of the local ironworks was owned by William Penn, founder of the state of Pennsylvania in the USA. St Laurence's Church stands in the oldest part of the village, known as The Moor. The great treasure of the church is its Great East Window, constructed around 1350, which has been described as one of the finest pieces of architecture in the country; the glass was replaced in 1956.

GOUDHURST, THE CULPEPERS TOMB 1904 52540

SPORTING KENT

The Vine Cricket Ground at Sevenoaks is possibly the oldest cricket ground in England, and was the site of the first cricket match ever to be reported in the national newspapers when a match took place there between Kent and Sussex on 9th September 1734. It was given to the town in the late 18th century by the 3rd Duke of Dorset of Knole, the great house near Sevenoaks, 'to be a cricket ground for ever'.

The St Lawrence cricket ground in Canterbury has been home to Kent County Cricket Club since the 19th century. For many years a famous feature of the ground was a large lime tree that grew within the area of the playing surface, unique in English county cricket. Sadly, the tree blew down in early 2005, during winter gales, but the cricket club had planned for such an event and had already begun growing a replacement, planted by the legendary Kent CCC cricketer Colin Cowdrey (1932-2000). One of the greatest batsmen to have played for Kent and England, Colin Cowdrey was the youngest player ever to appear in a match at Lords when he turned out for his hometown of Tonbridge in 1946 at the age of just 13 – and took 8 wickets in the match. Four years later he made his debut for Kent County Cricket Club, where he remained a player until his retirement in 1976 and led Kent to the County Championship in 1970. He captained England 27 times, and was one of the few batsmen to have scored over 100 first-class centuries. After his retirement he was involved in the administration of the game at county, national and international levels, and was made a life peer for his services to cricket.

Post-war Sandwich benefited from the development of nearby Sandwich Bay with its trio of golf courses, most notably the Royal St George. Founded in 1887, this course is widely regarded as one of the finest in the world, and regularly hosts the British Open Golf Championships. The famous writer Ian Fleming often frequented the Royal St George, which he wrote about under the name of Royal St Mark's as the setting for the memorable game of golf between James Bond, 007 and Auric Goldfinger in his book 'Goldfinger'.

The famous motor racing circuit at Brands Hatch near Swanley began as a dirt track motor racing circuit on Brands Farm. It hosted the British Grand Prix 12 times between 1964 and 1986. The first British Grand Prix at Brands Hatch was won by British racing driver Jim Clark, and the last in 1986 was also won by a British driver, Nigel Mansell, who holds the outright lap record for the Grand Prix course of 1:09.593. The full Grand Prix circuit has sections named after famous names in motor racing such as Cooper Straight, Graham Hill Bend and Brabham Straight. Brands Hatch also has a shorter 'Indy' layout. The Brands Hatch circuit hosts a variety of race meetings and championships, including the FIA World Touring Car and Formula Two Championships, British GT Championship and the British Superbike Championship.

The Tunbridge Wells Half Marathon each February is one of the South-East's leading road races, with around 2,500 entrants, and is a recognised 'pre-London' event. Run over a circuit through Tunbridge Wells and some nearby villages, 'Runner's World' magazine said of it that 'The historical villages and the undulating course make for a great race'.

SEVENOAKS, CRICKET ON THE GREEN c1960 S98042

QUIZ QUESTIONS

Answers on page 52.

1. Several towns in this book are mentioned as being one of the Cinque Ports – what does this mean?

2. What is the distinction between the appellations of 'Men of Kent' and 'Kentishmen'?

3. Why is there a statue of the Native American princess Pocahontas in St George's churchyard at Gravesend?

4. Faversham in Kent is advertised as the home of Britain's oldest brewer still in business – what is the company's name?

5. The West Kent Regiment gained the nickname 'The Dirty Half-Hundred' during the Peninsula War against Napoleonic forces on the Iberian peninsula of 1808-14 – why?

6. On the village green at Offham, west of Maidstone, is what is claimed to be last quintain in Britain. What is this, and what was it used for in the past?

7. Canterbury is often called 'the Mother of England' because its cathedral is the mother church of the Anglican communion throughout the world, but the city has also been referred to as 'the Midwife of America' – why?

8. What is the name of the famous play about the killing of Archbishop Thomas Becket in Canterbury Cathedral in 1170, and who wrote it?

9. What is known as 'Kentish Fire'?

10. Maidstone's coat of arms features a most unusual creature – what is it?

CANTERBURY
THE CATHEDRAL
BELL HARRY TOWER
1888 21359

RECIPE

ANGELS ON HORSEBACK

Whitstable's spacious harbour was opened in 1832 as the port for Canterbury, seven miles inland. Whitstable is famous for its oysters, and holds an oyster festival in July. A dish enjoyed locally is the Whitstable Dredgerman's Breakfast, consisting of fried streaky bacon cooked with shelled oysters, accompanied with thick bread and butter and a mug of strong tea. This recipe using oysters makes a delicious snack or appetizer. It dates back to Victorian times, when oysters were both plentiful and cheap, an everyday dish that everyone could afford.

> 16 oysters, removed from their shells
> Fresh lemon juice
> 8 rashers of streaky bacon with their rinds removed
> 8 small slices of bread
> Butter
> Paprika, or a dash of Tabasco sauce (optional)

Pre-heat the oven to 200°C/400°C/Gas Mark 6.

Sprinkle each oyster with a little lemon juice. Lay the bacon rashers on a board, slide the back of a knife along each one to stretch it and then cut it in half crosswise. Wrap a piece of bacon around each oyster and secure with a wooden cocktail stick. Arrange the bacon-wrapped oysters on a baking sheet. Put the oysters and bacon into the pre-heated hot oven and cook for 8-10 minutes. Whilst the bacon and oysters are cooking, toast the bread. When the bacon is cooked through, spread each slice of hot toast with butter, and place a bacon-wrapped oyster on top of each piece. Sprinkle with a little paprika or a dash of Tabasco sauce, if used, before serving.

RECIPE

KENTISH CHERRY BATTER PUDDING

Cherries are believed to have been introduced into Britain by the Romans and Kent was once famous for its cherry orchards. Sadly cherry production has declined in Kent nowadays because harvesting the fruit is such a labour-intensive business, but the traditional cherry dishes still survive.

> 3 tablespoonfuls of kirsch (a cherry brandy – optional)
> 450g/1 lb dark cherries, pitted
> 50g/2oz plain flour
> 50g/2oz caster sugar
> 2 eggs, separated
> 300ml/ ½ pint milk
> 75g/3oz butter, melted

Sprinkle the kirsch, if used, over the cherries in a small bowl, and leave them to soak for about 30 minutes. Mix the flour and sugar together, then slowly stir in the egg yolks and milk to make a smooth batter. Stir in half the melted butter, and leave for 30 minutes.

Pre-heat the oven to 220°C/425°F/Gas Mark 7. Pour the remaining butter into a 600ml (1 pint) ovenproof dish, and put the dish in the oven to heat.

Whisk the egg whites until stiff, then fold them into the batter with the cherries and kirsch, if used, and pour the mixture into the baking dish. Bake for about 15 minutes, then reduce the oven temperature to 180°C/350°F/Gas Mark 4 and bake for a further 20 minutes, until golden and set in the centre. Serve hot, sprinkled with sugar, with custard or cream.

QUIZ ANSWERS

1. The Cinque Ports were a medieval federation of ports which had a duty to provide the king with a number of vessels for his use for a certain amount of days each year, thus forming an early naval force. In return, the port towns enjoyed certain privileges, as well as a considerable degree of self-government. The original Cinque (pronounced 'Sink') ports were Sandwich, Dover, Hythe, Romney and Hastings, but in later years there were at least 25 towns connected to the Cinque Port Federation.

2. 'Men of Kent' and 'Kentishmen' are terms used for male inhabitants of Kent depending on where they live in regard to the River Medway. To the east and south of the river they are 'Men of Kent', whilst to the north and west they are 'Kentishmen'. Women in all parts of the county are known as 'Maids of Kent' after Joan, the 'Fair Maid of Kent' (1328-85), the daughter of Edmund of Woodstock, 1st Earl of Kent, who was known for her great beauty. She married the Black Prince, the eldest son of Edward III, and was the first English Princess of Wales.

3. The Native American princess Pocahontas is famous for saving the life of Captain John Smith during the early settlement of Virginia, by throwing herself over his body to prevent him being clubbed to death by her father's warriors. In 1614 Pocahontas became a Christian, taking the name of Rebecca, and married John Rolfe (1585-1622), another Virginian settler, who brought his wife and their young son to England for a visit in 1616. They stayed in England for nearly a year, and Pocahontas was presented at court to James I. However, she became unwell and died on a ship anchored off Gravesend as the family were returning to Virginia, and was buried in the vault below the chancel of St George's Church in the town. Her burial is recorded in the parish register for 21st March 1617, although her name was given as 'Rebecca Wroth', a 'Virginia Lady'. St George's Church was destroyed by fire in 1727 and rebuilt, and the location of her grave is no longer known. The statue of Pocohontas in St George's churchyard was erected to her memory in 1958.

4. Faversham is the home of the Shepherd Neame brewery, producer of traditional cask ales such as Canterbury Jack and Bishop's Finger Kentish Strong Ale.

5. The West Kent Regiment was the 50th Regiment of Foot – hence the nickname of 'Half-Hundred'. They gained the nickname of 'The Dirty Half-Hundred' after a battle during the Peninsula War because when the men wiped away sweat from their faces with the cuffs of their uniform jackets, they left smudges of black dye on their faces. "Not a good-looking Regiment, but devilish steady," said Sir Arthur Wellesley, Duke of Wellington, of the West Kents in 1808.

6. A quintain is a pole with a swinging arm which was used for jousting practice in the Middle Ages. One end of the arm was hit with a lance from a galloping horse and the other end would swing round, knocking the knight off his horse with a heavy weight if he did not ride out of the way fast enough.

7. In 1620 a Canterbury grocer called Robert Cushman led the negotiations at an inn in Palace Street in the city to hire a ship, the 'Mayflower', to transport the first group of religious and political dissenters known as the Pilgrim Fathers to the new colony of Massachusetts in America. Robert Cushman himself sailed on a later ship, the 'Fortune', and arrived in the New World in 1621. He returned to Canterbury a short time later to promote the colony's interests, and died there in 1625, but his son, Thomas Cushman, remained in Massachusetts where he became a ruling elder of the congregation at the Plymouth settlement.

8. 'Murder in the Cathedral', by T S Eliot. It was first performed in 1935 in the Chapter House of Canterbury Cathedral.

9. Kentish Fire is the name given to a particular pattern of hand-clapping in which two slow claps are followed by three quick ones, repeatedly. Its first recorded use was at a mass demonstration on Penenden Heath at Maidstone against the 1828 Catholic Emancipation Bill.

10. Maidstone's coat of arms features an iguanodon – a large dinosaur – because the remains of an iguanodon were found during quarrying in the Queen's Road area of Maidstone in 1834; the remains are now in the Natural History Museum in London. Maidstone is the only local authority in Britain with a dinosaur supporting its heraldic arms.

FRANCIS FRITH

PIONEER VICTORIAN PHOTOGRAPHER

Francis Frith, founder of the world-famous photographic archive, was a complex and multi-talented man. A devout Quaker and a highly successful Victorian businessman, he was philosophical by nature and pioneering in outlook. By 1855 he had already established a wholesale grocery business in Liverpool, and sold it for the astonishing sum of £200,000, which is the equivalent today of over £15,000,000. Now in his thirties, and captivated by the new science of photography, Frith set out on a series of pioneering journeys up the Nile and to the Near East.

INTRIGUE AND EXPLORATION

He was the first photographer to venture beyond the sixth cataract of the Nile. Africa was still the mysterious 'Dark Continent', and Stanley and Livingstone's historic meeting was a decade into the future. The conditions for picture taking confound belief. He laboured for hours in his wicker dark-room in the sweltering heat of the desert, while the volatile chemicals fizzed dangerously in their trays. Back in London he exhibited his photographs and was 'rapturously cheered' by members of the Royal Society. His reputation as a photographer was made overnight.

VENTURE OF A LIFE-TIME

By the 1870s the railways had threaded their way across the country, and Bank Holidays and half-day Saturdays had been made obligatory by Act of Parliament. All of a sudden the working man and his family were able to enjoy days out, take holidays, and see a little more of the world.

With typical business acumen, Francis Frith foresaw that these new tourists would enjoy having souvenirs to commemorate their days out. For the next thirty years he travelled the country by train and by pony and trap, producing fine photographs of seaside resorts and beauty spots that were keenly bought by millions of Victorians. These prints were painstakingly pasted into family albums and pored over during the dark nights of winter, rekindling precious memories of summer excursions. Frith's studio was soon supplying retail shops all over the country, and by 1890 F Frith & Co had become the greatest specialist photographic publishing company in the world, with over 2,000 sales outlets, and pioneered the picture postcard.

FRANCIS FRITH'S LEGACY

Francis Frith had died in 1898 at his villa in Cannes, his great project still growing. By 1970 the archive he created contained over a third of a million pictures showing 7,000 British towns and villages.

Frith's legacy to us today is of immense significance and value, for the magnificent archive of evocative photographs he created provides a unique record of change in the cities, towns and villages throughout Britain over a century and more. Frith and his fellow studio photographers revisited locations many times down the years to update their views, compiling for us an enthralling and colourful pageant of British life and character.

We are fortunate that Frith was dedicated to recording the minutiae of everyday life. For it is this sheer wealth of visual data, the painstaking chronicle of changes in dress, transport, street layouts, buildings, housing and landscape that captivates us so much today, offering us a powerful link with the past and with the lives of our ancestors.

Computers have now made it possible for Frith's many thousands of images to be accessed almost instantly. The archive offers every one of us an opportunity to examine the places where we and our families have lived and worked down the years. Its images, depicting our shared past, are now bringing pleasure and enlightenment to millions around the world a century and more after his death.

For further information visit: www.francisfrith.com

INTERIOR DECORATION

Frith's photographs can be seen framed and as giant wall murals in thousands of pubs, restaurants, hotels, banks, retail stores and other public buildings throughout Britain. These provide interesting and attractive décor, generating strong local interest and acting as a powerful reminder of gentler days in our increasingly busy and frenetic world.

FRITH PRODUCTS

All Frith photographs are available as prints and posters in a variety of different sizes and styles. In the UK we also offer a range of other gift and stationery products illustrated with Frith photographs, although many of these are not available for delivery outside the UK – see our web site for more information on the products available for delivery in your country.

THE INTERNET

Over 100,000 photographs of Britain can be viewed and purchased on the Frith web site. The web site also includes memories and reminiscences contributed by our customers, who have personal knowledge of localities and of the people and properties depicted in Frith photographs. If you wish to learn more about a specific town or village you may find these reminiscences fascinating to browse. Why not add your own comments if you think they would be of interest to others? See **www.francisfrith.com**

PLEASE HELP US BRING FRITH'S PHOTOGRAPHS TO LIFE

Our authors do their best to recount the history of the places they write about. They give insights into how particular towns and villages developed, they describe the architecture of streets and buildings, and they discuss the lives of famous people who lived there. But however knowledgeable our authors are, the story they tell is necessarily incomplete.

Frith's photographs are so much more than plain historical documents. They are living proofs of the flow of human life down the generations. They show real people at real moments in history; and each of those people is the son or daughter of someone, the brother or sister, aunt or uncle, grandfather or grandmother of someone else. All of them lived, worked and played in the streets depicted in Frith's photographs.

We would be grateful if you would give us your insights into the places shown in our photographs: the streets and buildings, the shops, businesses and industries. Post your memories of life in those streets on the Frith website: what it was like growing up there, who ran the local shop and what shopping was like years ago; if your workplace is shown tell us about your working day and what the building is used for now. Read other visitors' memories and reconnect with your shared local history and heritage. With your help more and more Frith photographs can be brought to life, and vital memories preserved for posterity, and for the benefit of historians in the future.

Wherever possible, we will try to include some of your comments in future editions of our books. Moreover, if you spot errors in dates, titles or other facts, please let us know, because our archive records are not always completely accurate—they rely on 140 years of human endeavour and hand-compiled records. You can email us using the contact form on the website.

Thank you!

For further information, trade, or author enquiries
please contact us at the address below:

The Francis Frith Collection, Unit 6, Oakley Business Park, Wylye Road, Dinton, Wiltshire SP3 5EU England.
Tel: +44 (0)1722 716 376 Fax: +44 (0)1722 716 881
e-mail: sales@francisfrith.co.uk **www.francisfrith.com**